12 21. 19

Dear Wonder,
    You are ...
friend and inspiration..
    I adore you.

            Rochelle

Are These My Hands Now?

Aging and Me

Rochelle Turoff Mucha PhD

In Loving Memory of my Mother,
who aged with extraordinary grace.
An ideal I have yet to achieve.

Contents

Musing 1

Becoming Invisible 3

    Senior Discount Day 7

    My Mother Would Love Those Shoes 11

    You Look 61! 13

    We Have Stairs 15

    Because You Are Getting Old 17

    Eligibility 19

Discerning Reflections 23

    Mirror, Mirror on the Wall 25

    The Dressing Room 27

    My Hands 29

    Familiar 33

    Do I Look Like Anyone? 35

Seeking Liberation 37

    A Picture Says a Thousand Words and More 39

    Going Natural 41

    Laughter 45

    Dancing the Night Away 49

    Women Rising 51

    To Hear or Not to Hear 55

I Am Too *Old* for This... 59

Me and My Shadow(s)..61

Still Becoming 65

Telling Your Story 69

My Attitude.. 71

Becoming Invisible...73

Discerning Reflections......................................75

Seeking Liberation...77

Age

Noun ** Verb ** Adjective

To Come of Age

Act Your Age

Ageism

Aged Well

Aging Population

Ageless Beauty

Musing

I am turning seventy this year. The number does not scare me. It has been an amazing journey.

I should not be surprised that the academic in me who yearns for facts and the behaviorist in me who covets reflection and introspection appear to be colluding, compelling my preoccupation with the aging process.

I see *age* everywhere I go, and with everyone I meet.

The young woman jogging ahead of me while I walk. *Does she appreciate those smooth cellulite-free thighs?*

The older stranger at a restaurant. *Does she know her dyed hair may make her look older rather than younger?*

The senior flight attendant. *Does she feel less attractive than the majority of her younger colleagues?*

The elderly woman slowly moving forward with her walker. *Does she long for days past, or was she always slow to move?*

The group of familiar female faces of my family, friends, and neighbors I have watched slowly don the signs of aging over the decades. *Do they see the same?*

Is this book merely a collection of my contemplations with the aging process?

Are these vignettes and reflections commiserative, amusing, informative, or inspirational?

You decide.

Becoming Invisible

The Lady Vanishes, a 1938 Alfred Hitchcock suspense masterpiece, is one of the greatest train movies from the genre's golden age. It tells the story of a spinster, a passenger on the train, who abruptly vanishes. We see her briefly as she etches her name on a misty train window, each letter swiftly evaporating. A younger woman is troubled by her disappearance but fails to find anyone else on the train who saw her. All the younger woman can recall when asked to describe the older woman is that she was "middle-aged and ordinary." In truth, she can't remember her. As the story unfolds, the missing woman seems to be a figment of the imagination with no real characteristics. Laughter, tension, and eccentric characters entwine to captivate the audience until the final scene when the missing woman's true identity as a British spy is disclosed, and she materializes as the film's bona fide heroine.

How apt that an eight-decade-old movie has emerged as a metaphor for discourse about aging women and their unique challenges. It is, in part, a comedy, and yet there is nothing laughable about the legitimate feelings many older women harbor of being overlooked, rendered invisible.

Literally, to be invisible is not to be seen. To feel invisible is to perceive we are being ignored, not taken into consideration. Too frequently, the aging perceive ourselves as invisible. For as long as we are alive and kicking, we are literally seen, hence making the distinction between literal and perceived critical.

When any older person is disregarded, reduced to caricatures, aging becomes anathema to every person. Aging isn't easy on anyone, but much of the data indicate it is even more challenging for women than for men. "Invisible Woman Syndrome" is one of several catchall phrases created to label and explain why women in their forties and fifties seem to disappear from public view. Although easy to see this played out on television, film, and theater as some of our favorite female actors lose out to younger women for leading roles, this syndrome impacts women across all walks of life. The invisible woman may be the shunned actor after her fortieth birthday, the fifty-year-old struggling to secure a job interview, or the sixty-year-old divorcee flummoxed by the lack of responses to her online dating ad.

Search the internet and you will find countless stories testifying that the feeling of not being seen is acutely felt by middle-aged women and beyond. A plethora of academic and self-help publications have flooded the market to illuminate this topic. Sadly, the feeling of being invisible is directly tied to the ongoing and persistent societal double standard of women defining themselves and their worth by their physical appearance. For many women, the core of feeling old, invisible, or ignored is undoubtedly connected with the loss of attractiveness. Men no longer eye you up and down when you walk into a room or indulge you with seductive, flirty looks. The sultry but delicious feelings innocent coquetry engendered within us go extinct.

The significance of physical appearance for both sexes has always been different. For men, attractiveness is an advantage. For women, it is expected. Men have physiques that imply size, strength, or athleticism. Women have figures alluding to shapeliness and sexuality. Men are hunks, toned, and authoritative. Women are thin or voluptuous, diminutive or desirable.

Factually and anecdotally, the natural physical changes that accompany aging for both genders impact women more than men, and that means it is harder for women to find new jobs, lovers, and even friends.

Being valued for what women look like in place of what women do or have done sounds superficial because it is. However, if we scratch deeper into that objectification, we realize that the feelings of loss are more far-reaching than physical vanity in our later years.

I recently watched a documentary about Supreme Court Justice Ruth Bader Ginsburg. She was eighty-four at the time of the filming. I was stunned by the images, swagger, and confidence of the young Ginsburg, a beautiful, feisty, determined woman who grew to be a giant of personality and power. I was struck that I only knew of her as the demure, tiny, and oldest sitting Supreme Court justice. Without the back story, even a woman of such stature can be largely invisible. When we meet someone in her closing chapter, maybe that is all we see.

I feel invisible as I age because people I meet don't know me. They don't know who I am or how I came to be seventy years old. They don't know my story, my struggles, my accomplishments.

I feel invisible because I am stereotyped into a class of people, a club I have not yet willingly joined. My individuality and my value seem irrelevant.

I feel invisible because I stay silent and polite, even when I want to scream to make myself seen and heard.

Becoming invisible exposed my vanity, and that frightened me. Capturing those moments in print allowed me to find humor, insight, and comfort, empowering me to strive toward liberation.

Perhaps this can be the case for you too.

Senior Discount Day

Publix Supermarket is one of my neighborhood stores. A few years back, I was eager to take advantage of its Senior Discount Wednesdays, a benevolent nod to the aging that offered a whole 5 percent deduction from my bill—until the day I loaded my groceries on the conveyor belt and the clerk said something like, "I've included your senior discount."

What! No request to see my driver's license to verify I was truly 62 or older?

I *look* old. I do not have to *prove* it. No mistaking me for a spry gal in her forties.

My discount giddiness soon morphed into melancholy. I look my age. Maybe I look even older.

There are a myriad of discounts for people over fifty. Movie theaters, restaurants, hotels, rental car companies, retail operations, supermarkets, and museums all offer senior discounts. Even many local governments offer age-based real estate tax exceptions.

Typically, there are conditions and variables. Initiation can be fifty, fifty-five, sixty, sixty-two or sixty-five. I guess we are not sure when people are old enough. Your senior discount may be restricted to specific days of the week or particular times of the day. That early bird meal is timed perfectly; it comes before the hip crowd dines and ensures you can get home in time for an early lights out. Tuesdays and Wednesdays are slow retail days, so the aging are encouraged to flock to the stores on those days, helping to justify big box overhead and staff.

Senior discounts are controversial in some circles. They started in the 1930s during the Great Depression when our older population became disproportionately poor compared to other age groups. For many, a lifetime of savings vanished in a flash. Today, those days and data no longer hold true. Yet habits are hard to break, and senior discounts persevere.

Currently, the most poor and vulnerable age group is our millennials. There are those who think senior discounts should be a thing of the past, and we would better serve our community if we helped our struggling young people instead. There are others who claim rewards for being old are disingenuous because they are not a form of respect or honor. If you truly want to help seniors, give them something they need, like adding vision, hearing, and dental coverage to Medicare, all of which are not included in our core health plan. Equally important, hire seniors instead of tossing their resumes and dismissing them sight unseen solely because of their age.

Curiously, despite the potential savings, many seniors do not take advantage of senior discounts. Doing so would be indisputable evidence they are getting old. Paying full price is often preferred.

Hmm, I have noticed that I avoid Publix on Wednesdays.

I remember when...

Supermarkets were a great place to meet men. After all, everyone shops. I moved to Maryland in 1976. One Sunday morning I whisked off to the supermarket in shorts, T-shirt, no makeup. I met a guy who lived in New Orleans. It was instant chemistry. That chance meeting led to a rendezvous in the Big Easy. Guess that will never happen again.

My Mother Would Love Those Shoes

I suffered a spontaneous and severe hip fracture when I was forty-nine, the painful outcome of having osteoporosis before Fosamax was on the market. Not because Fosamax would have helped me (my bones were in bad shape) but because a medical doctor may have known what to do when an osteoporotic patient came in with a hairline femur fracture. Instead of sending me home, maybe they would have known to put me on crutches or bedrest. Before Merck was making boatloads of money on Fosamax, osteoporosis was an invisible disease to most, but not to me.

Now, twenty-one years later, I go for a bone density test every five years. As you likely know, it is a noninvasive procedure that causes no pain or discomfort. You would think they would figure out how to do this in lieu of the regular mammogram that annually makes me, a fairly small-busted woman, feel like a Mack truck has descended on my boobs.

When my name is called I depart the waiting room and follow a friendly technician who confirms my identity and takes me into the exam room—a mindless activity so far. I follow directions, lie on the table, and await the moving box above me that will measure my bone health.

Midway through the exam the technician says, "Where did you get those sandals?" "France," I happily reply.

"My mother would love those sandals."

Your mother, I say to myself. *Not you—your mother?*

Shock hits me first. *I look like your mother? Maybe I should have put on some makeup and styled my hair today.*

Denial follows. *These sandals are way cool. Take a closer look. Can't you see the silver and pink? How can you think these are shoes for old women? They are nothing like those big, strappy, clumsy things so many women wear.*

Anger emerges. *Do you need glasses? Are you competent to do this test? Do you know how good I look for my age? Everyone tells me so.*

Guilt rises. *Why am I angry? Of course she knows how old I am. My birthdate is on my chart. It's possible this is a compliment in disguise.*

Acceptance settles in. *I am seventy. My feet are in good form, not misshapen. I am being too sensitive. This is about me, not her. I should be flattered, not offended.*

All this sounds trivial, but in the moment it was huge. I was wearing sandals her mother would like. I felt old. I was literally, and ostensibly, fashionably old enough to be her mother.

I remember when...
I flaunted a red-sequined bandeau to a company party, dispelling my colleagues' conservative assumptions about me. I wore short shorts, midriff tops, and craved provocatively low-cut dresses. Now I scour the shelves for clothes that obscure my droops, dimples, and creases. Clothes as seduction is a bygone era.

You Look 61!

I was nineteen when I married, and I was twenty when I became a mother. Never much for makeup, trendy clothes, and hairdos, I was carded at R-rated movies to prove I was at least eighteen, the minimum age required for entry.

When I would take my toddler son for a walk, the guys hanging onto the Brooklyn sanitation trucks would often shout, "Taking your brother for a stroll today?"

When he was in high school, he towered over my five-foot-three-inch frame as I attended his football reception. Later, his friends teasingly told him he must have been adopted because I was too young to be his real mom.

When I took my adult son to a nice restaurant for dinner, he worried people would think he was a cougar hunter.

I loved each indulgent moment of looking younger than I was. It was fun—an unintentional masquerade I reveled in.

Then a conversation with a new friend changed all that. Just about any first date begins with lots of small talk about life and family. It often goes like this:

Me:
My son is forty-nine.
She:
What? Wow!

Me:

My granddaughters are seventeen and fifteen.

She:

You are kidding me!

Me:

My oldest granddaughter is looking at colleges next semester.

She:

Get out! OMG.

Me:

I will be seventy in April.

She:

You look sixty-one.

Sixty-one. *Is that supposed to make me feel good?* I am not sure what sixty-one looks like. Better than seventy, I guess.

I don't feel sixty-one. I feel thirty, maybe forty or, on an achy day, fifty. Older people report that they feel an average of thirteen years younger than they literally are. She could have at least told me I looked fifty-seven. I gather I just have to reconcile the duality of looking one age and feeling another. It is what it is.

I remember when...

My sister was visiting me and we went to Wolf Trap, a fabulous outdoor theater outside of Washington, D.C. Midway through the performance I started feeling ill: hot, sweating. I wound up in the emergency room with a fever of 105. Not good. The aide who rolled me from the ER to my room was trying to make small talk. Reading my chart, which clearly stated my age, he cheerily told me, "I can't believe you're forty. You look twenty-five." I smiled, charmed, and I basked in the flattery. Those days are now far behind me.

We Have Stairs

My husband and I were on a mission to find two new reclining chairs for our living room. I had bought him a great looking recliner when we got engaged. (That was my second marriage, and I was fifty-one, ergo, the practical engagement gift.) Now eighteen years later, the chair had seen its better days. It took me a good deal of convincing to get him to let go of his special chair. It helped that I gave it to a neighbor and friend who allows my hubby to go down the street and sit in it when he is feeling nostalgic.

We searched all over for the perfect recliner—not too big, not too small, not too clunky. He is six feet plus, so it also had to fit him without swallowing me up.

One time we entered a two-story Pottery Barn. I had seen a chair on its website that looked like it might work. We approached a salesperson on the main floor and asked where we could find that chair. She answered, "Second floor. The elevator is over there."

I gather we looked like we would need or want an elevator. Sigh... We walk three miles a day. I am confident that was much more than the salesperson did.

That salesperson, with the best of intentions, made assumptions about our physical needs and spoke to us in a patronizing manner. She is not alone.

Researchers call such language "elderspeak," an approach that treats older people more as children than fully functioning adults. People might slow their speech, raise their volume, or talk in sing-song sentences. That is especially true in health care settings.

The response to a photo or video of older folks singing, dancing, or engaging in sports, activities they have done their entire lives might provoke adjectives such as "precious" in a similar way the sight of kittens, puppies, or babies does.

When my husband and I take our customary walk out of our neighborhood and through the park, we hold hands. Countless numbers of strangers in cars and on foot stop to tell us that we are "adorable." *Why are we more adorable than a young couple?*

Our graying temples seem to elicit unrequested assistance with door openings, luggage handling, entering and exiting vehicles, navigating stairways, and the like. Though such gestures may be compassionate, they are not always welcomed. They feel presumptive. They make me feel old.

Here is a news flash: we are getting older, but we still curse, lust, aspire, and prize our independence. When we need help, we will let you know.

I remember when...

I took two buses every day to get to and from my newlywed apartment to Brooklyn College. I was pregnant during my senior year and relatively large. Buses were crowded, and often I would stand for both rides. Nobody ever got up to offer me a seat. I presume aging prompts more attention than pregnancy.

Because You Are Getting Old

When I turned sixty I noticed a theme that unfolded from nearly every doctor visit, whether it was routine or special.

At the end of an eye exam, the somewhat timid optometrist would mention some minor changes and caveat her remarks with, "You know, it's all part of the aging process."

The dental hygienist noted concern about potential bone loss, shifting teeth, and decay, predictable declines that accompany advancing birthdays.

A visit to a back specialist after I emerged from a kayak in sharp pain yielded a diagnosis of spinal stenosis and a shrug that seemed to say, "What else should you expect at your age?" The number one cause of back pain is disc degeneration, a byproduct of aging.

Wincing in pain to close a bra, pull up leggings, or reach across the front seat of my car required me to visit the shoulder guy. I learned that atraumatic rotator cuff tears in the elderly (sixty-five years and older) are normal. The doctor cheerfully explained that although he usually would not consider surgery for anyone my age, he would make an exception in my case. I assume I should have felt flattered. I was not. Backs, shoulders, hips—I reckon knees are next. I am unequivocally falling apart.

I always had a lot of hair, not thick, but plenty of it. So after months of monitoring a thinning patch of hair that was expanding on the top of my head, I went to see my dermatologist. He blamed hormone changes and casually chanted the all-too-familiar post-menopause mantra. Evidently, another freebie of aging is that hair follicles no longer work effectively to allow for hair growth. On the plus side, my once spaghetti straight hair is now wavy.

Even the ordinary post nasal drip is not spared. A lingering nuisance during the prime of your life can turn into a constant nag. As you age, it seems the tip of your nose droops and the columella, the bridge of tissue that separates the nostrils at the nasal base, retracts, culminating in decreased air flow. That condition, combined with reduced hydration, exacerbates and elongates the symptoms associated with the common cold, allergies, and hay fever.

I get it. The aging body is, well, aging. The whole shebang gets worse as we grow older. But when the default diagnosis, the root cause of all our ailments is our rising age, I think health professionals are less likely to see anything else. In fact, comorbidities (commingling disorders) are prevalent in older people, and the typical diagnostic method—"law of parsimony" (the simplest explanation)—health professionals employ frequently does not apply.

At a time in our lives when our need to be "seen" is most crucial, we may truly be most invisible.

I remember when...
I felt like a whole person rather than just an old person, a stockpile of deteriorating parts.

Eligibility

A while back my son embarked on a travel adventure. It was in part a sponsored trip made possible by an organization seeking to strengthen its participants' religious/ cultural values and traditions. His wife was an enthusiastic member. Though skeptical at the onset, he returned transformed.

Even I, an agnostic, felt a tinge of envy when he shared his stories and new-found faith. I was so moved that I googled the organization, eager to see what transformational experiences I could take advantage of. The answer was none. A basic requirement to enroll was that you needed to have children at home under the age of eighteen.

At first that requirement perplexed me. Then it annoyed me. But the more I thought about it, the more it made sense. *Why invest in a person seventy years old with adult children, grandchildren, and whose exit was nearer than further?* If the goal of the organization was to deepen affiliation, folks my age and those who were childless were useless. That started me thinking about other offers and promotions.

I was exploring dental practices on the internet as part of my search for a new dentist. I was taken aback by all the new patient offers and discounts. *Are these dentists truly eager to have me as a new patient?* People in their final life stage would not present the same promise of longevity that grabbing a young family or a millennial might. Given my lack of long-term value, those dentists might just foist their least experienced professionals on me. That's why I'm probably staying with my current dentist; growing older together is a better, safer idea.

Much of my shopping is digital. Launch any cosmetics or fashion company web page and the image that will greet you is young, very young. Despite the fact that I spend good money on such products, those sites are definitely not in search of me. Even cruises, which largely cater to and are supported by our aging demographic, populate their sites with youthful canvases.

All of that appears to be in conflict with factual trends. By 2047 it is projected that there will be more people over sixty than under fifteen. People are living longer, are healthier and, although their monthly income may decrease, their overall wealth and discretionary income may increase. A substantial segment of our aging community spends more on travel, dining, and new cars than any other age group, so that seems like a missed opportunity for marketers.

What I receive instead are countless ads for anti-aging products, soothing walk-in tubs, scooters, medical alert systems, funeral guidance, slip-free floor pads, and a phenomenal array of other gadgets for the elderly as well as a weekly invite for a gratis retirement meal-planning event. Those are the products marketers think I want today.

Children can feel overlooked, cast aside, invisible in an adult world. For all we know, that feeling could simply be the natural order of things, aging and becoming invisible again.

I remember when...

I was a target customer for new trends, part of the sought-after audience companies competed heavily for. I felt wanted. I yearn to see vibrant seventy year-olds when I click on the retail or travel link I am searching for as opposed to the negative aging stereotypes that fill my screen with merchandise that keeps reminding me how old I am.

Discerning Reflections

For some people, shopping is sport. Not for me. It is more like travel entertainment.

I enjoy the adventure of shopping when I travel, browsing in and out of small boutique stores, exploring what gifts I might purchase, what knickknack I will add to my array of travel keepsakes. (When you are in a second marriage, you buy gifts for your home, not your children.)

When I wander leisurely down quaint streets to assess storefronts of various sizes and their contents to determine which to enter and which to pass, I cannot help but glimpse my reflection, my silhouette.

But wait, who is that?

The reflection I see does not look like the woman I feel.

Not straight. Too wide. Too many bumps. The face looks different. *Are those my jowls?*

I feel thirty, but my reflection is seventy. *How can that be?*

I know I am aging but intellectually, socially, and emotionally I remain on intimate terms with my younger self. The reflection I see now is surreal; it's as if I am gazing at myself from a distance and seeing a woman I know, but not well.

The dissonance between how we feel as we age and what we see in our reflection can be daunting. Tom Hussey, an advertising and portrait photographer, created an award- winning series of conceptual photographs titled *Reflections of the Past*. His work was inspired by an elderly veteran who found his personal image virtually unrecognizable.

Reflections of the Past presents older people conducting mundane tasks while pensively looking at their younger, more appealing selves in a mirror and seeing images of them when they were in their prime. There is a woman at a dressing table alongside the reflection of her career as a nurse; another is reminiscing about her wedding day; another is performing her first piano recital. The photography captures wistful, rapt, poignant moments that deeply connect the eyes of the present with a treasured past.

Reflections bombard me wherever I turn. I want to embrace the woman in the glass, but it is hard. I am not ready—yet.

I remember when...

I had a habit of practicing my next age immediately after my birthday. As soon as I turned twenty-nine, I was already saying I was thirty. I think doing that somehow softened the milestone, or maybe it just felt playful because I always looked younger than my age. That practice stopped at sixty-nine. Seventy sounded like a number I could wait for.

Mirror, Mirror on the Wall

Nowadays, avoidance is the only word that comes to mind when I think of mirrors. I catch a brief look of myself and quickly turning away as if doing so eliminates the image I don't identify with. (My vanity mirror is an exception. My ten times magnification is the only way I can put on makeup.)

I am not alone.

Nora Ephron knew that feeling too, and in *I Feel Bad about My Neck,* she expressed it like this: "That's another thing about being a certain age that I've noticed: I try as much as possible not to look in the mirror. If I pass a mirror, I avert my eyes. If I must look into it, I begin by squinting so that if anything really bad is looking back at me, I am already halfway to closing my eyes to ward off the sight."

Nora Ephron, bless her soul, was wonderfully witty. I am just a regular person.

There are mirrors everywhere.

Stores.

Bathrooms.

Elevators.

On the rare occasion I am in the back seat of a vehicle, an unavoidable peek at myself in the rearview mirror is depressing. I want to duck, but there is no escape.

The mirror that hangs over my closet door can be horrifying. A pair of jeans I wore only a few months before are too tight now. I stare at my body in disbelief. It is chunky, newly defined by uninvited bulges and rolls. There is no denying that my body no longer measures up to the ideal shape I worked so hard and so long to achieve. I am eating the same. I exercise daily. Despite my efforts, my figure has changed without my permission, surrendered to metabolism. *What happened to that young girl? Where is the woman I feel like?*

Looking in the mirror sometimes leaves me feeling betrayed, like an innocent victim. The images seem distorted. They must be. That reaction may be completely irrational, but it feels true nonetheless. I note a deep pang of loss and, at the same time, a deep pang of guilt.

When will I be free from the self-imposed torment of the mirror? When do I arrive at acceptance?

I do not know.

I remember when...

I was perusing an old photo album, the kind we had before we went digital. I was smiling in a dozen or so pictures as I showed off a new, voguish hat. I was having fun with the camera, expressing my sense of style and play, entertaining myself. That was then. Now, no Face Time shots or selfies for me.

The Dressing Room

Even as a young girl, I did not like getting undressed in front of others. When my family visited a public beach with public locker rooms I would squirm and search for a corner, for any privacy as I squeezed in and out of my wet bathing suit.

I don't remember ever undressing in front of my first husband. I would hole up in the bathroom and then come out in my not-so-sexy PJs.

I thought my behavior must have been because I was chubby, plumper than most of my friends. I was physically shy, embarrassed.

When I found myself at twenty-four a divorced, single mom and an unexpected ten pounds slimmer, my reflection became my friend. My shyness yielded to comfort. For the first time in my life I genuinely liked the way my body looked.

Then, it changed.

Of all the reflections I see, the one in the typical dressing room is most harsh.

There is no place to hide in a dressing room. There are no human shields to block your view. The mirror is inescapable. The fluorescent light is unforgiving.

When did my skin begin to resemble crumpled napkins, my stomach refuse to stay flat no matter how hard I suck it in, and when did the cellulite spread to my arms and elbows?

Shopping in stores became unbearably painful, something to evade at all costs. Lucky for me, that feeling coincided with the exponential rise of online retail. I cultivated a new habit. If I needed or wanted something, I would purchase several options online, have them delivered, try them on in the privacy of my own bedroom, and return the items I did not want. I could dodge the dressing room and, it turns out, have considerably more options to choose from on the web.

I remember when...

I was in Cancun with a boyfriend. I was twenty-six and bikini thin. He took a photo of me on a boat in my black bikini. As a former chubbette, I was reluctant to acknowledge that the girl in the picture was me. Unlike now when I steer clear of seeing my image, then I could not stop looking, scrutinizing the photo, certifying that it truly was me. Though that was our last jaunt together, I still keep that photo in my jewelry box, a reminder of days, and a body, past.

My Hands

When my oldest granddaughter turned four, her celebration was held at a nail salon. At that age, grandparents were still invited to birthday parties. All those little four-year-old girls marched into the salon and knew exactly what to do. They went to the trays of nail polish to explore and select their favorite colors (frequently more than one each) and then confidently sat at the manicurist's table. I found that experience an enlightening observation of changing times.

I think I had my first manicure when I got married—the first time—at nineteen. I know I was in my fifties before manicures and pedicures became habits. Until then I found giving myself a manicure and pedicure relaxing—a complete, mindless diversion.

I will blame my second husband for converting me into a regular. I made the mistake of insisting he get a pedicure while on a beach vacation early in our marriage. Pity the poor technician: fifty-five years of callouses. My husband liked it—too much. He started joining me on my occasional visits to the local salon. Over time, with increasingly poor vision and back issues, occasional became regular.

When you get a manicure you become a captive audience of your hands, monitoring the process to ensure the shape is right, and you prevent getting nipped by a slip of the cuticle scissors.

The technician works with a strong light guiding her. Age spots. Wrinkles. Sagging. Dryness. Bulging veins. Prominent joints. *Are these my hands now?*

Aging has no mercy on our hands:

- Knuckles swell
- Hands lose volume, expose tendons, and allow veins to protrude
- The number of capillary loops decline, leading to impaired circulation and susceptibility to the cold
- Elasticity weakens, resulting in wrinkles and sagging
- The aggregate of sensory receptors decreases and, consequently, diminishes tactile sensation
- Years of unpreventable sun exposure lead to discoloration and crepiness

Throughout our life span, our hands are the parts of our body that are most exposed to stresses and injuries, so it is not surprising that our hands are a visible, telltale sign of our age. We can fix our face, but we better keep our aging hands in our pockets or wear gloves.

As my manicurist works her magic, my veins emerge above the surface, and age spots freckle my arms, undeniably reminding me how old I am, how the years have taken their toll.

I remember when...

I went shopping with my first husband for my first engagement ring. My finger was a size four. I had lovely, long, thin fingers. Enviable hands. I look back with pleasure on how I have used my hands to convey my feelings through affectionate hugs, gentle strokes of someone I love, or my thoughts as I typed a document or flipped a page of a book that enraptured me. And now I also see my hands as living witnesses to seven decades.

Familiar

On the first day of my first year of college I met my first college boyfriend, Artie. He was a downright funny guy. On our first date he picked me up at my apartment. That would be my parents' apartment, the two bedroom, one bath unit I grew up in and from where I commuted to Brooklyn College daily.

Back to the date. The doorbell rings and Artie enters. I introduce him to my parents, Artie takes a long look at my mother, and he says, "Not bad if this is what you will look like when you are older." Like I said, a funny guy.

Truthfully, then it felt great. My mom was thirty-five when I was born, making her fifty-three to my seventeen the night of that first college date. She was an attractive woman with great skin. Being told I might look like her when I grew old felt like a compliment.

When we are young, it is hard to imagine that one day we will resemble our aging parents. That realization is not necessarily a cause for elation. Nevertheless it happens, and it is not surprising if we are products of their DNA.

Some friends were at a baseball game when, during one of the breaks between innings, the camera swept the stands and projected close-ups of the fans. When my friends' picture showed up on the screen, one of them looked up and innocently announced, "My parents are here!"

I have those moments when I glance briefly at my silhouette and literally stop, startled at the thought that I'm seeing my mother—a split second that stirs unexpected memories.

Photography is one of my husband's hobbies, and when we travel that hobby becomes an obsession. He takes an abundant number of pictures. My efforts to shun his camera are largely unsuccessful. The headshots of me that I like best are when my head is perched at an angle, usually on a boat or a beach, and my hair is in the wind, freely enjoying the disorder caused by an ocean breeze.

I started to print and frame those photos, a literal line-up, unknowingly creating a living chronology of my aging process. The aging face I see resembles my mother's. Seems like Artie was right.

I remember when...

I became a mother and read lots of parenting books and articles. Frequently, there would be quotes from parents exclaiming they couldn't believe what they were saying or doing, that they sounded and acted just like their parents. For all we know it is subliminal that we become our parents when we parent, and so it may be that we can experience a preview of our older selves by simply looking at and listening to our parents.

Do I Look Like Anyone?

My older sister cringes when I tell this story, but it is true.

Our father played in weekly card games throughout our childhood. When he hosted, other men would fill our small apartment for rounds of gin rummy or pinochle. Cigar smoke would envelope me. There was no dodging the noise, the odors, or the men.

My sister was exceptionally beautiful, striking. She was innately fashionable and swank. One time I remember a family friend and card player proclaiming that she looked just like Elizabeth Taylor, the gorgeous movie star. I whimpered and pleadingly asked him, "Who do I look like?" No reply. I desperately wanted to look like someone too, preferably someone pretty.

That scenario led me to conclude I was not pretty, ever. Instead, I was the smart one. As hard as I might try to be snazzy, I felt doomed to mediocrity when it came to attractiveness.

I was rummaging through an old photo album recently in an effort to label the pictures with names and dates and places so that whoever might view them one day would know what they were looking at.

There I was in one collection, age three to thirty. Staring at each image, sorting out times and locations, I realized, for the first time, that I had been pretty and not fat, just as my mother used to reassure me.

I was the lively school girl, carefree and cute, playing with her friends; the nineteen-year-old bride, blissful and winsome; and the new mother, bright-eyed and vivacious. The vignettes smiling at me were, indeed, beautiful. *Why had I believed otherwise?*

I wince when I think back on a lifetime of self-imposed doubt and insecurity, wasted time and energy. Maybe when I am eighty and look back at my seventieth birthday pictures I will marvel at how young and pretty I was.

I remember when...

I was teaching preschool. It was my first job, and I loved my toddlers. My son, conveniently, attended the same school. It was the early 1970s. Annie Hall *was a big film, and Diane Keaton was Woody Allen's favorite gal. I showed up at work one day with a big floppy hat, and one of my student's parents declared, "Oh, my, you look just like Diane Keaton!" I had arrived. Finally, I looked like someone.*

Seeking Liberation

I was a single mother living paycheck to paycheck for one third of my working life. If my car broke down, it could bring me to tears, but it would not defeat me. I pushed through those circumstances without knowing where I was pushing to.

I refused to allow the toxic people in my life to define me or drag me down to their level.

If I got fired from a job I liked and/or needed, I would shop for something frivolous to prove nothing could thwart me.

If I didn't get chosen or invited, I would not let the rejection determine my view of the world or my degree of happiness.

Why am I letting aging and ageism get to me? Why am I pouring out my thoughts, observations, and reflections?

Because how we age is a choice. We can lament or rejoice. We can stagnate or grow. We can submit or prevail.

Because what we think dictates how we feel, and if we are to feel more positively about our aging process, we need to think differently about it and talk differently about it.

I want to make a conscious decision to unchain myself from the shackles of aging, to accept my years and welcome my next phase—physically, emotionally, and socially. I don't want aging to dictate my attitude, my aspirations, or my confidence. I want to promise myself to age gracefully with poise and courage by following my heart and mind, not the mirror.

I realize all of that is easier said than done, but embracing the fact that aging is merely another aspect of living, of being human, is powerful. Recognizing that aging is unstoppable, and appreciating that our individual experiences are both universal and subjective is liberating.

I have traveled a long way, and most of the roads were not paved. I want to value the journey that has brought me to how and why I look and feel the way I do.

I envision...

My future in which, each day, I seek to debunk the stereotypes of older women and stand tall and proud, exercise daily, travel to new places, play often, learn sign language, and master the piano.

A Picture Says a Thousand Words and More

By now you might have guessed that I have framed photos all around my house. My shelves and closets are bursting with albums. My life, and the lives of those I love, greet me daily. Together they comprise a silent but animated family history.

I was born in 1949. It is unlikely my parents owned a camera then. The sole infant photo I have of myself is a professional shot. I found it when my mother died, and now I keep it propped up on a table in my office. There are three poses, and I am adorable (everyone is adorable at six months) in each one—lying on my belly, sitting up with my rattle, gesturing with my little hands, "Who, me?"

I take it on faith that the baby I am looking at is truly me. I search for similarities. My eyebrows, the shape of my nose, the happy smile. Hard to know.

Through the many images that surround me I chart my growth, my evolution as a person and as a woman.

School photos show me how I grew. Once taller and in the back line of class pictures, in later grades I moved to the front. Must have been an early growth spurt because I ended up petite.

As I age from child to woman, the shape of my body develops from straight and flat to curves, hips, and breasts. I am thinner, then chunkier, then thinner again.

I watch my profile slowly change through life-cycle celebrations. Birthdays, weddings, grandchildren, bat mitzvahs. I see myself grow older, but I also see sameness—the way I pose my head, place my hands, the direction I look when I sit or stand.

A lifetime of photos captures my changing fashion tastes and trends. The clothes! *What was I thinking?*

But nothing is more hilarious than my hair. Anyone else looking at this chronological collage would never think this woman is the same person. I even have trouble recognizing that fact myself.

Straight spaghetti hair through childhood. Then there were bangs. It was frosted at nineteen for my first wedding, and then I cropped it really, really short after our honeymoon. I grew pigtails by the time I became a mother at twenty.

Brown hair. Red hair. Highlighted. Curly. Page boys. Very long and then short again.

Apparently I never loved my natural hair. Time to change that!

I envision...

The pictures to come, watching with delight as my granddaughters graduate from college and begin their adult lives, celebrating my son as he enters the second half of his first century, welcoming great-grandchildren, and exploring the world—snapshots that will confirm the deepening of the lines in my face and the wisdom and love in my heart.

Going Natural

Perceptions about hair color may be the deepest and most entrenched double standard that defines aging. A graying male is seen as distinguished, successful, even sexy— free to age with abandon. A woman, in contrast, fears looking like her grandmother and frets over what others will think. She's terrified of enduring a horrific transition to her natural hair color.

I propose that women bear the burden for why this bias remains so strong.

In 2014, prior to my oldest granddaughter's bat mitzvah, I experienced an epiphany. For most of my adult life I had colored my hair. First, as a relatively poor single mom, I would retreat to the shower every six weeks and use an over-the-counter product to liven up my naturally soft, brown hair. I wanted to be blonde, but mostly I was peroxide orange. Then, when I achieved middle class, I started to go professional. By the time I was sixty-five and no longer working, my quarterly highlights were costing $250 a pop. Enough!

I made the decision to go natural.

Beyond hair color being too expensive, I had started to notice my peers, those in their sixties, seventies, and eighties who continued to color their hair. And a good deal of what I saw I did not like.

Hair, like skin, ages. In addition to losing melanin that causes natural graying, dipping keratin protein levels leave hair weaker, less elastic, dull, thinner, prone to breakage, and less voluminous. Continuing a regime of coloring, heat drying, and excessive use of hair products is like adding fuel to the fire for fragile, aging hair.

Hair encircles our faces and, as we age, facial skin grows more delicate, paler, more translucent, and more subject to pigmentary changes. Some of the older women I saw who were still coloring their hair looked like their hair did not match the rest of them.

I did not want to look like that. And I did not want to, nor could I afford to, keep up the salon routine. I am confident I am not the only woman resenting the effort and expense.

I cut my hair short to expedite a process that can be long, awkward, and terrifying. Lo and behold, when it was complete I had the most beautiful highlighted gray hair at no cost. And to think I had spent thousands over the years for that effect.

I know I was lucky. I began with no expectations. I took a leap of faith, and my hair grew out looking tremendous, even to me.

During the process, and even after it, what irked me was people's comments. "You let your hair go gray?" *No, I let my hair go natural.* "What does your husband think?" *Do you know anyone who asks a man if his wife approves of his graying hair?* I don't think so.

Going natural was one of two most liberating moments in my life. Unfettering myself from the encumbrance of hair color and the expense and anxiety over my appearance was incredible, almost too fantastic to put into words. I felt beautiful. I felt proud.

Why do most women persist in coloring their hair when most men do not?

Why do women reinforce society's premise that men with gray hair are sophisticated, but women with gray hair are old?

In this situation, women are their own worst enemy. This is a double standard that we, as women, must control.

I envision...

My hair becoming completely white. I will be ready!

Laughter

**We don't stop playing because we grow old;
we grow old because we stop playing.**
– Oliver Wendell Holmes

A vivid memory comes to mind of when I became engaged for the second time and was planning our intimate wedding. I was browsing through invitations in search of a lively, not-so-serious design when the owner of the store approached me. She asked why I was getting married again. "Among other things," I said, "he makes me laugh." He did, and he still does.

Laughter is important at all stages of our lives. In celebration and in defeat, laughter lifts our spirits, sets us free, beams us up and up and up. The presence of laughter breeds an optimistic attitude, and the absence of laughter proves detrimental to our well-being.

It is not surprising that there is a positive relationship between laughter and aging well. A healthy sense of humor helps us acclimate to our age, influences our varied relationships, and increases individual satisfaction. Research reports that laughter boosts immune function, pain tolerance, cardiovascular health, and maybe even memory retention.

Laughing at losses and unchangeable circumstances enhances our situation by releasing painful emotions and normalizing experiences. Do you recall Norman Cousins' *Anatomy of an*

Illness in which he shares how he fought and won his battle with a life-threatening diagnosis with the power of laughter? "Ten minutes of genuine belly laughter," he wrote, "had an anesthetic effect and would give me at least two hours of pain-free sleep." His book became a catalyst for decades of research on the role humor and laughter play in our health and welfare.

Humor is subjective. Whether you get a hoot out of late night television, sitcoms, or stand-up is not the salient point. Whatever makes you chuckle is great. Most of us have witnessed how laughter can get us through the toughest times. Therefore, retaining a sense of humor as we age is imperative.

In the course of writing this book I learned about the Red Hat Society, a playgroup created in 1998 to connect like-minded women, foster friendships, and enrich lives through the power of fun. The organization has chapters across the country, and some are exclusive to women fifty and older. The Red Hat Society encourages women to be outrageous, or at least to feel like they are. The society was inspired by Jenny Joseph's poem "Warning," widely known for this opening line: "When I am an old woman I shall wear purple" and "with a red hat which doesn't go and doesn't suit me." The Red Hat Society costume includes purple attire along with the red hat, buoying members with rallying cries of "Why wait?"

Laughter is fundamental to the human experience and, as we age, a playful spirit can mediate challenges and diffuse our fears. Perhaps laughter is the best medicine.

I envision...

Those special moments when uncontrollable laughter will spur tears to stream down my cheeks. My husband mimics me when I lose it to laughter. He exaggerates, or not, the weird sounds coming from me when I am doubling over engulfed with funny. I am thankful for laughter.

Dancing the Night Away

I love to dance. When the music starts I am the first one on the dance floor. For me, dancing is freedom to move, to feel, to create. It is a visceral experience.

In my thirties and forties I took up tap, attending class twice a week. The sound of precision tap, its energy and musicality, were thrilling.

Dance is a beautiful way to communicate and connect; it's a form of personal expression. The magic of dancing in sync with others is potent, and swaying in step with a partner is sensual.

Dance is a window to our emotions. There is the intimacy of a waltz, the passion of the tango, the nostalgic exuberance of the Charleston.

It makes sense that dancing is beneficial at any age.

Dancing is physical, fortifies bones, strengthens balance and flexibility, and improves cardiovascular health. Dance as therapy uses movement to facilitate physical, cognitive, and emotional integration. Dancing also reduces stress by stimulating emotional and physical release.

What you may not know is that dancing has an anti-aging effect on the hippocampus region of our brains. That region controls memory, learning, and balance. Research has confirmed that learning and memorizing dance steps, patterns, formations, routines, and associated movements keeps our hippocampus in shape more so than endurance training.

My husband's son recently got married. We were on the dance floor the whole night, moving to the music with no constraints. Younger folks said they were impressed by our stamina. We were told we were an inspiration. When the wedding photos were published there we were, dancing in every frame, seventy years young.

I am baffled when someone says they can't dance. Of course they can. Maybe not like Fred Astaire, but who can? Dancing is as natural as communicating, which we all do even though many of us aren't good at it. That lack of ability does not stop us. My husband put up a fuss at first, preferring to sit it out, brooding about his two left feet. Today he dances unencumbered by his previous fear of embarrassment.

Moving is good for the body and mind, so get your dancing shoes on, shake a leg, and give your brain a boost.

I envision...

Being the first and last person on and off the dance floor. In the spirit of Lee Womack's wonderful song, dancing is a metaphor for taking chances, trying something new. It is about living fully, and it can be liberating. So, "When you get the choice to sit it out or dance. I hope you dance."

Women Rising

A female centenarian was asked, "What is the best thing about being one hundred three years old?" She smiled before replying, "No peer pressure."

It could be that at one hundred three the competitive pressure fizzles. As desirable as that may be down the road, it may not be reassuring for those us who are a few decades her junior.

There has never been a level playing field for women and men, but as we age that polarity intensifies as more women are pushed out, marginalized, or overshadowed by a culture that worships youth and beauty. While a man's value can soar with age like a fine wine, a woman's usually plummets. Men in their fifties are still advancing their professional and sexual prowess. Conversely, many of their female peers are fading into the background, invisible, considered past their sexual prime and usefulness.

Granted, some things have improved, but not as much as they need to. Women with the same qualifications as men often earn less and are less likely to be promoted. Although women are the majority gender, equally educated and credentialed, there are far fewer female medical school deans, university presidents, law firm equity partners, and CFOs in Fortune 500 companies than men.

Ageism irrefutably intersects with sexism. Combined, they dole out a double whammy, devaluing women for the perceived loss of power and beauty, two key levers in American society.

By the end of January 2019, the year I began to write this book, several high-profile stories were busting barriers about aging and women.

- Susan Zirinsky was announced as the first woman to lead CBS News. Moreover, at sixty-four, she was the oldest person to assume that role.

- Nancy Pelosi, seventy-eight, was reelected Speaker of the House of Representatives, making her the most formidable elected woman in US history.

- Representative Maxine Waters became the first woman and first African American to lead the Financial Services Committee. She's eighty.

- Glenn Close, seventy-one, prevailed over four younger women to win the Golden Globe and SAG awards for best actress.

- Christiane Amanpour, sixty, was selected to replace the anchor on a prime-time PBS interview show.

- Representative Donna Shalala became the oldest female freshman in her 2018 House class when she took office several weeks before her seventy-eighth birthday.

Those achievements demonstrate real progress and are cause for optimism.

According to the US Census Bureau, there are more women over fifty in this country today than at any other point in history. These women are healthier, work longer, and have more income than those of previous generations. The landscape of women's working lives is changing, and with that change comes an opportunity for all of us to stand up and not be cast aside, wherever we are.

When we compete to retain our youth and succumb to traditional pressures, I suggest we are colluding in our own disempowerment. When we extricate ourselves from the misery of worrying about our looks and our age, it's liberating.

The women's movement in the seventies urged us to seize our power. Now, pro-aging movements will help us hold onto it. Be part of the movement! Be seen, be heard, and be relevant.

I envision...
A time when my teenage granddaughters and their peers and partners will grow older gracefully without being troubled about their looks or their age, that they will prosper and thrive for all their years equally with the men in their lives.

To Hear or Not to Hear

Approximately one in three people between the ages of six-ty-five and seventy-four has difficulty hearing, and that percentage grows to fifty percent for those older than seventy-five. Age-related hearing loss—they even have a name for it, presbycusis—occurs normally, a near certainty as we age. Illness, medications, accidents, and overexposure to loud noises or music (rue those disco days!) are additional causes of hearing loss.

Hearing is a fluid process. Sounds entering the ear canal cause the eardrum to vibrate. Those vibrations move through three little bones called the ossicles to the cochlea, causing its fluid to move. That movement, in turn, prompts tiny hair cells in our inner ear to move, creating sound waves that are converted into neural signals that are transmitted to the brain, which interprets them as sound.

When those little hair cells are healthy they appear to be lined up, standing tall in a row. When they are damaged, they look like wilted flowers. There are two groups of hair cells; one sends low-pitched sound information and the other high pitched. Once damaged, or dead, a range of sounds might be lost, no longer encoded and transmitted to the brain. That explains why hearing loss may seem selective.

The hair cells are a critical path to our auditory nerve, and when they are not functioning properly, all the other structures in the pathway are negatively impacted, compromising the entire system. Ordinarily, those hair cells regenerate, but when we reach a certain age, they do not reproduce and, subsequently, hearing loss becomes permanent.

This is not a lighthearted topic. When people who have enjoyed full hearing their whole lives begin to lose that hearing, they can become lonely and socially isolated. There are studies that report a link between hearing loss and cognitive decline, even dementia. Missing out on conversations, the ringing of the doorbell, and even the sounds of traffic is stressful.

My story is a little different. I have been completely deaf in my left ear since I was eight. For sixty-two years I have learned to accommodate that serious loss.

Growing up in a Brooklyn tenement, being deaf on one side was an advantage. If I turned over and slept on my good ear, the perpetual street noise would be silenced.

When I was working with a client group, I would let them know in advance that if they were sitting on my left side they would have to be more creative in capturing my attention. I was not ignoring them. I simply could not hear them.

Single-sided deafness often held benefits for the men in my life too. I advised them if they had something sweet to say, speak into my right ear and be rewarded. If they had something nasty to say, opt for my left ear, and they would avoid punishment.

Because of my hearing loss, sitting in the passenger seat in a car forced me to twist my neck to hear. That's why I frequently volunteered to drive.

Choosing seats in a restaurant or theater could feel like a game of musical chairs. I switched from one seat to another, seeking the most ideal hearing position, strategically placing the person I needed to hear from the least on my left.

As a single-sided deaf person, a typical hearing aid would not be helpful. There was nothing to amplify. Then things changed. Technology advanced, and the BiCros was invented. I could get a device for my deaf ear that would receive and forward sounds to my hearing ear. The decision to go forward with the device should have been a no-brainer. I should have been jumping for joy. But I wasn't.

During my visit to the audiologist my resistance materialized as excuses. The hearing aid was too expensive, which it was. *Would the benefit justify the cost?* The hearing aid manufacturers were unethical. *You can trade in or upgrade your automobile, so why not your hearing aid?* The device was not all that small. *Maybe I should wait a few more years.* I have been doing fine for sixty-two years. *Why change?*

Honestly, I did not want a BiCros. Only thirty percent of people who could benefit from hearing aids use them. Much of the reason driving the remaining seventy percent to pass stems from the stigma associated with hearing loss. The core of this stigma revolves around changes in our self-perception, vanity, and ageism, and it is heard and seen in a variety of ways.

Younger folks whine in frustration about needing to repeat themselves to their aging parents and grandparents and older colleagues. Being blind elicits more patience and empathy than hearing loss. Advertisements for hearing devices emphasize appearance rather than quality of life. Few insurance companies cover the cost of hearing tests or devices, implying hearing aids are not essential health devices but merely nice options.

Wearing a hearing aid is physical evidence of the gap between your former and current self, between being abled and disabled. It is a badge that you are aging, an uncomfortable thought that may generate concern about losing younger acquaintances. Fear of being classified as handicapped deters action. The notion that wearing a hearing aid is unattractive and will draw conspicuous attention weighs heavily on decisions.

It is no wonder we resist hearing aids. *Who wants to volunteer to be uncool? Ugly? Old? Burdensome? Stupid?*

More often than not, the unfortunate consequence of all those factors is that struggling with a hearing loss seems a better alternative than getting help. The truth is a hearing aid would improve your life, not worsen it. Because you can hear better, you can participate fully, respond appropriately, eliminate asking people to repeat themselves, minimize anxiety associated with avoidance, retain your social life and/or career and, most importantly, keep your brain working at full capacity.

For my seventieth birthday I took a test drive with a BiCros hearing system. I kept asking my husband to whisper into my deaf ear to see if I could accurately hear what he was saying. I could. It was remarkable. It felt miraculous!

To hear or not to hear? If that is the question, my answer is easy—to hear.

I envision...
The day when hearing aids become as trendy and chic and competitive as eye glasses.

I Am Too *Old* for This

Unquestionably, aging goes hand in hand with some annoying, even frightful realities as it entails the gradual loss of so many things we took for granted when we were younger.

That said, with age comes priceless wisdom about life and implications for how we should expend our energy and efforts. Our mortality looms surreptitiously in front of us, each day, each moment, and that means how we use them is consequential.

Dominique Browning published a first-person piece in which she expounds on her newly adopted mantra, "I'm Too Old for This." Much aghast, her younger friends advised her against using the word "old" and encouraged something softer, like "wise" or "smart." She rejected those comments and proudly boasted she had earned the right to "old." *Haven't we all?*

There is something inherently liberating about exclaiming aloud or to yourself, "I'm too old for this!" (Credit to Dominique Browning for inspiring the liberations below.)

Many of us have spent years feeling insecure about our looks and perceived inadequacies. No feature was spared. We were too short. Too tall. Too thin. Too fat. Had big feet. Little feet. Pudgy fingers. Skinny fingers. Were flat chested or bosomy... It feels like we have been worrying about our bodies and appearances most of our lives.

I am physically changing, and there is nothing I can do about it. I may not be able to wear the most fashionable clothes and shoes, but my body is fit, able, and energetic.

So what if I have taken to wearing tunics and blouses that cover my butt. I declare I am too "old" to be bothered by bone-thin models and fashion trends that render me invisible.

Toxic, thoughtless, rude people—those who will drag me down with regrets or endless complaining—will have to find an ear elsewhere. I declare I am too "old" to pretend I can change anyone, and I have precious little time left to spend with bitter folks. That includes me. No whining, spoken or unspoken. I'm better off pumping my heart with a long walk.

The world and its list of troubles—politics, climate change, economics, health care, education—grows longer and more overwhelming every day. Once I was ready to debate it all and often. Now I opt to say I am too "old" to combat every issue or pretend I can fix things that I can't.

What matters most is right now, seizing every day and every opportunity to live fully. Life is messy at any age. The only difference is what you do with the mess. Resiliency is the key to feeling young and living well. I am too "old" to do otherwise.

I envision...

A time when the insights we derive as we age are available to those who are young. Cliches are cliches for a reason: Youth really is wasted on the young.

Me and My Shadow(s)

I have not aged alone. I have been accompanied by family, friends, and colleagues, some transient and some for the duration.

It all begins with my mother who strikingly wore her hair straight back in a ponytail during my toddler years. Next came a transition to a shorter bouffant hairdo and, ultimately, in her later years, to an easy-to-manage cropped pixie. All the while her hair color changed from brown to gray to white. Her skin was natural and flawless till her eighties. She was never one for makeup. Only once did she share that the woman she saw in the mirror was a stranger, no longer the visage of the woman she knew. My mom aged with extraordinary aplomb, an ideal I have yet to achieve.

My sister, the fetching one, was also the testy daughter. Sharing a bedroom until she married we jostled under the covers, outgrew our metal, stand-alone clothes closet, and competed for privacy. Motherhood and divorce drew us closer. We traveled together, commiserating about loves and losses, celebrating life's milestones, and always—despite the distances between us—glued to a rock-solid foundation as sisters and best friends. Four years my senior, she still engages the room as she enters with great panache.

My son, the first true love of my life, entered the world the way he lives in it. Quick. Determined. Tenacious. Commanding. A playful, loving child, he has grown into an impressive and devoted man, husband, and father. He laments that now he is the oldest in his company and sometimes can't keep up with the late party hours he used to enjoy. He shaves his head rather than grapple with baldness. Next year he can join AARP.

My husband is my soul mate. After eighteen years together, his brown mustache is no longer brown. Although he has stubbornly relinquished major landscaping tasks to a professional, he clearly is immune to being bothered by age spots, thinning hair, or sagging muscles. Back surgery, and even a bout with sepsis, failed to hamper his love of birdwatching, photography, Sudoku, cooking, and absolutely silly jokes. I always knew he was a man I could grow old with, and I am.

Both my grandmothers were deceased before I was born. I never understood how that absence affected me until I became a grandmother myself. The gift of being a grandmother is truly magical and, in a way, inexplicable. The birth of a grandchild unleashes an unknown but anticipated euphoria, a jolt of happiness that feels like falling in love for the first time. With my granddaughters I have endless patience and am always present in the moment, ways of being that challenged me as a mother. Evidence of their life stages, toys, and projects adorn my home. Grandchildren happily melt your heart as well as your wallet, and I willingly surrender to their hugs, smiles, and obvious manipulation every time. Memories of cuddling with storybooks, cooking together, conducting science experiments and art projects, playing board games, and enacting make-believe scenarios are indelible. Watching them progress from house plays to school performances, dollhouses to babysitting, kindergarten to college, and bicycles to driving has been priceless. Hoping they live long, fulfilling lives after I am gone and that they might carry a little bit of me on their travels is comforting.

My husband's children were little people compared to my married son when I first met them. Recollections of teaching them, serving as an audience for their original choreography in the living room, discovering adolescent sites visited on the family computer, and traveling to baseball games delight me. I have watched them become young adults, professionals, husbands, and fathers, finding their way and place in the world.

My lifetime friends have moved from being caretakers to sometimes care receivers, work to retirement, single to married to grandmothers. We have shared decades of girl talk, secrets, dreams, laughter, and tears. Now they are filling new chapters of their lives with bridge, painting, and pickleball. We bemoan the problem of finding an affordable master on main, the strain of carrying our own luggage, the shoulders that can't quite hit that tennis ball or swim that lap as before. There are significant memories of work and play, heartaches and elations, angst and victories. There is gratification derived from decade-old relationships that cannot easily be described.

They all have contributed to the tapestry of my life, each person a cherished thread of a different color that created my cloth.

I envision...
Still becoming.

Still Becoming

Life should NOT be a journey to the grave with the intention of arriving safely in an attractive and well preserved body, but rather to skid in sideways, chocolate in one hand, wine in the other, body thoroughly used up, totally worn out, and screaming, 'WOO-HOO, what a ride!'"
– Hunter S. Thompson

As I grew older I began reading obituaries. It was not a morbid interest; it grew out of attending funerals where I came to understand that I actually did not know the person being buried. Most times I had met them toward the end of their lives, and it was only at their funerals, through stories, that I became acquainted with their adventurous, passionate, vibrant youth.

What stands out for me in obituaries is the repeated phrase "courageously battled." I wonder, *Do we courageously battle living as much as we apparently do death?*

I look back and believe that I have courageously battled to live a full life, a life I would not have been able to imagine when I was a teenager. As scripted as every day was for me through high school and my first marriage, my journey turned out to be a colorful quilt of unpredictable adventures and misadventures, often the road less taken, layered with unforeseeable hills and valleys.

I have lived through seven decades. I have been a daughter, sister, wife (twice), lover (frequently), mother, stepmother, grandmother. If I am lucky I will hold my great-grandchildren in my arms as I did both my granddaughters. I have buried two parents. I have observed and participated in a shifting society where technology has changed almost every aspect of our daily routines, and where sweeping progressive legislation has broadened the concept of inclusion only for it to suffer painful regressions.

We begin to age from the moment we are born. As we move through life's stages and milestones, it makes sense that the way we define ourselves and measure our self-worth should evolve over our life span. At a certain age, we should wrap up some weathered attributes of our younger selves in a box with a bow, replace them with new dynamic features, and cultivate new strategies for optimizing the promising years ahead.

Mary Pipher, prolific author of *Woman Rowing North: Navigating Life's Currents and Flourishing as We Age*, declares that seventy is an important birthday, a border. Possibly more pivotal than any other transition in our lifetime, seventy is the age to exercise our power of choice, to willfully choose our attitude to live our lives purposefully and to fervently reject settling for a diminished version of our younger selves. Aging well is intentional. It is about choosing to live fully into your eighties, nineties, and beyond.

My choice is to embrace my aging with gratefulness. For seventy years my arms have hugged many people in love and support; my eyes have seen a sea of faces; my ears have listened to melodies of voices and music; my legs have traversed diverse landscapes; my laugh lines embody the joy of family and friends. Gratitude is not optional, it is essential, it is comforting.

My choice is still to be "becoming," to continue to learn, adapt, thrive, and contribute; to be the best version of myself. I can't do that if I am horrified to look in the mirror.

We all have a story to tell and celebrate. Some memories delight us, and others elude us. Our minds and experiences are richer. Our connections deeper. Our self-knowledge keener.

We cannot go backward. We can only go forward.

I envision... tomorrow.

Telling Your Story

My chronicle began as an effort to speak for and to other women to illuminate our shared obstacles and opportunities. Through the years, personally and professionally, I have learned that I am good at expressing emotions and observations other people won't say. My intention was to be light-hearted and to let kindred spirits know they are not alone.

The writing process is emergent. This final product is, in part, cathartic self-therapy. Sobering data I discovered both informed and unnerved me. Resources surfaced that bolstered me. Humorous anecdotal tales unfolded that engendered levity.

What became increasingly clear to me was that the topic of women and aging is not only popular, but important to talk about and talk through.

I invite you to tell your story, to put to paper your thoughts and attitudes on aging, how and if you feel invisible, and to work through your reflections toward liberation.

My Attitude

Grappling with aging begins with knowing what biases and assumptions we bring to the aging process, so ask yourself the following questions and then answer them.

- Do you tell people your age?
- What do you like or dislike about your age? Why?
- What makes you see someone else as an old person?
- What does it mean when someone says, "I don't feel old"?
- Do you think there are certain clothes older women should not wear? Why?
- What are your opinions on anti-aging treatments? Why?
- What changes do you expect as you age? Physically? Mentally? Socially?
- What are your greatest fears about aging?

Becoming Invisible

Ask yourself the following questions and then answer them.

- What age do you feel, and what does that mean to you?
- If you feel old, when and why did you first feel that way?
- In what ways, if any, do you feel invisible? Where? With whom?
- Do you think you are treated differently than when you were younger? If so, how?
- What age are you, and how do you truly feel about that?

Discerning Reflections

Ask yourself the following questions and then answer them.

- Where do you see your image?
- What do you see in your reflection today?
- What feels familiar? What feels strange? What are your reactions?
- What does it mean when someone says, "You look great for your age!"?
- How does your age affect how you feel about your body?

Seeking Liberation

Ask yourself the following questions and then answer them.

- What actions can you take to liberate yourself from the fear and reality of aging? Who do you need for support?
- What and who are you grateful for?
- Where is the laughter in your life?
- What are you too "old" to be bothered by?
- Who is/are your shadow(s)?
- How are you, or how will you, still be "becoming"?